1

flip front cover

2

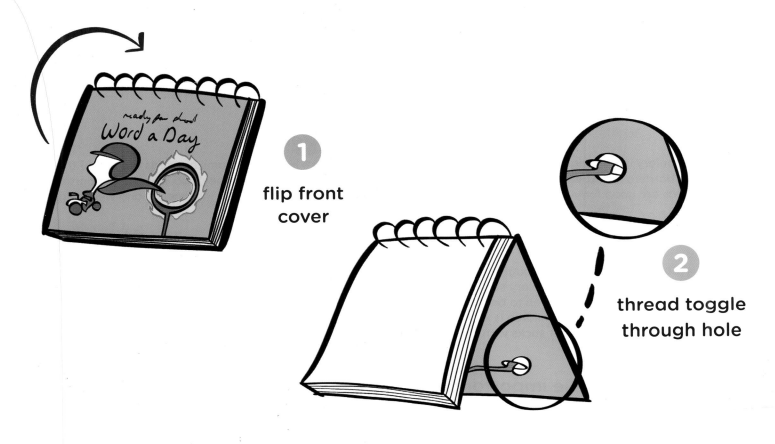

thread toggle through hole

Now, place the book on a surface, learn a word a day, and get r-r-ready for school.

Get started!

Who's who

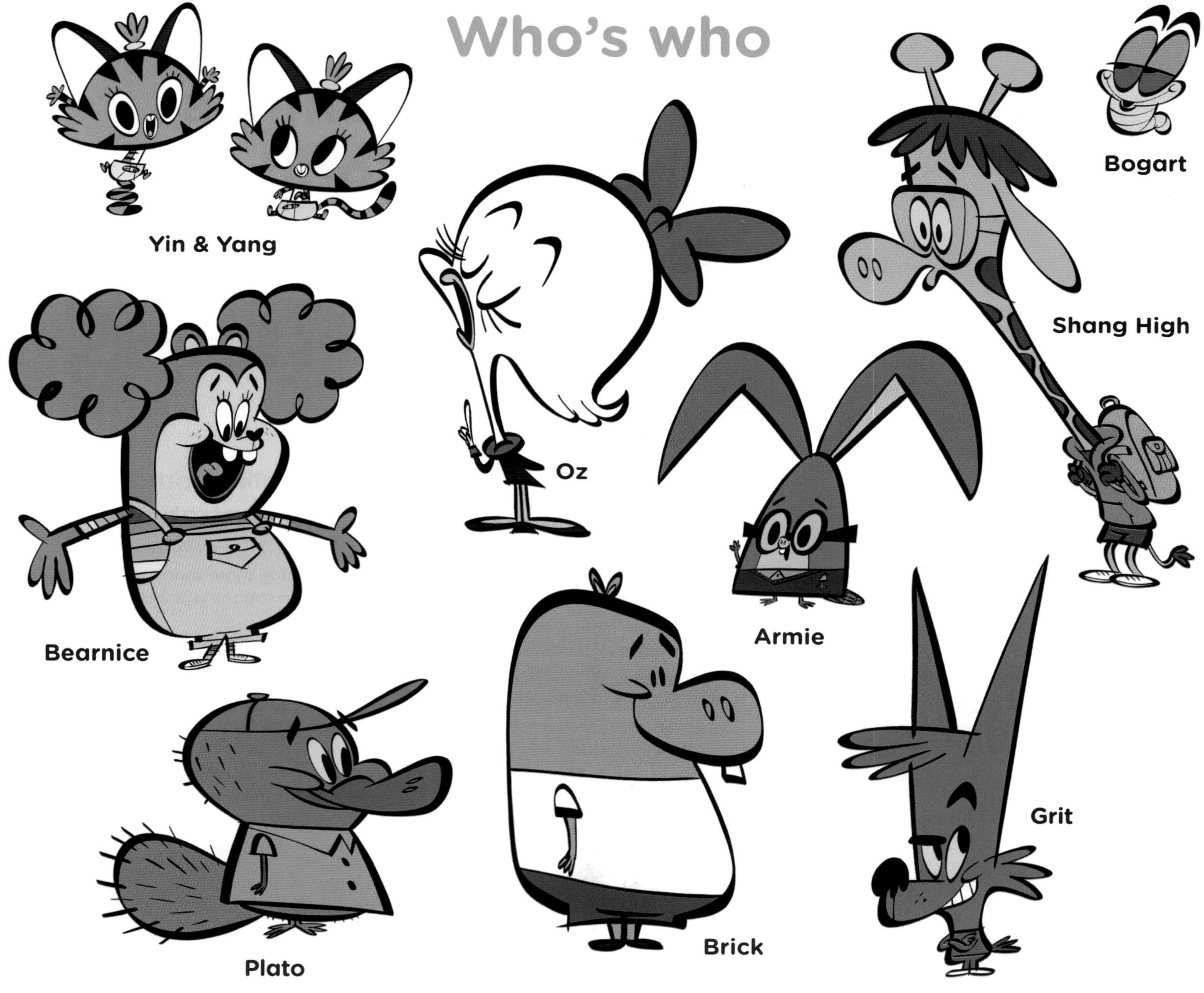
Yin & Yang
Bogart
Shang High
Oz
Bearnice
Armie
Grit
Plato
Brick

eat

to put something in your mouth, chew, and swallow it

Oz **eats** spaghetti for dinner.

mrswordsmith.com

hungry

how you feel when you want to eat

Yin feels so **hungry** that she points at her mouth.

mrswordsmith.com

starving

how you feel when you really need to eat

Grit is **starving** so he almost eats Plato's tail.

mrswordsmith.com

eat, sleep, and laugh words

thirsty

how you feel when you want a drink

Grit feels so **thirsty** that he will drink anything.

mrswordsmith.com

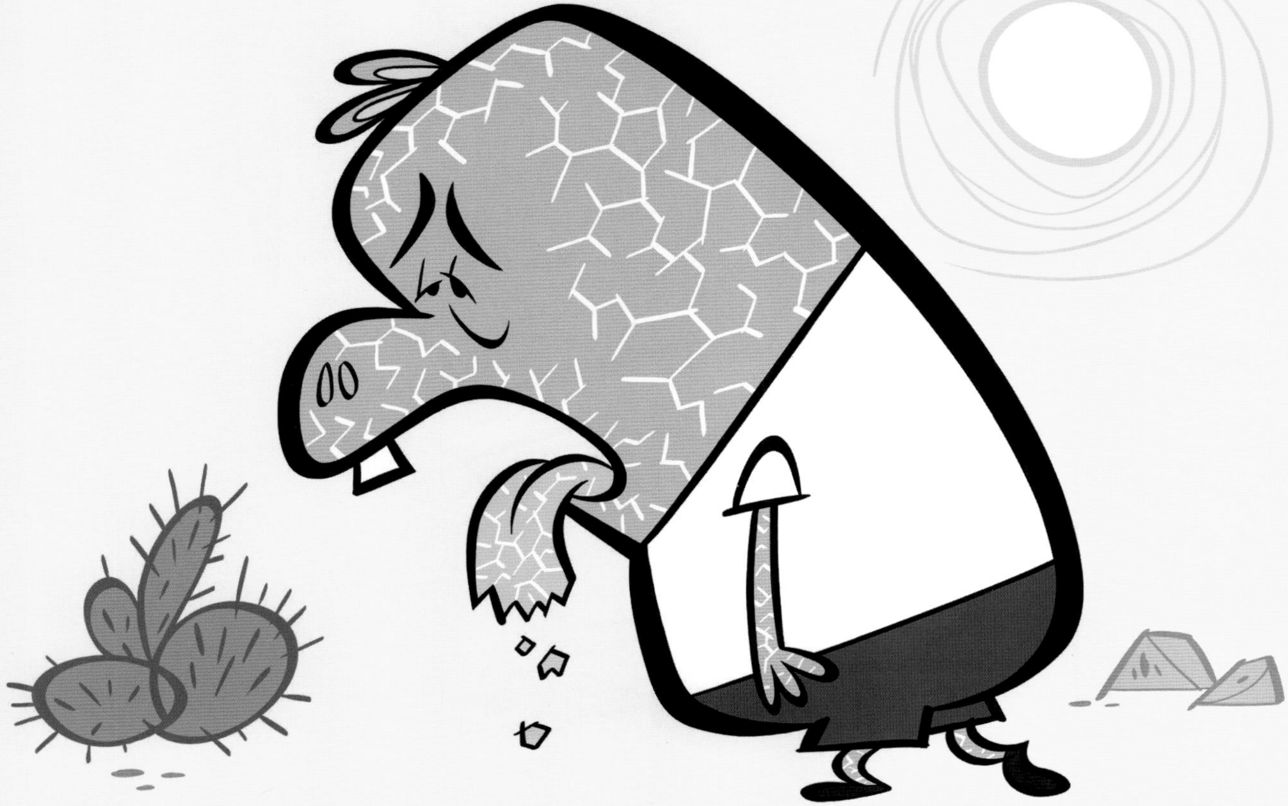

dehydrated

when you feel weak because you haven't had enough water

Brick gets **dehydrated** in the hot weather.

mrswordsmith.com

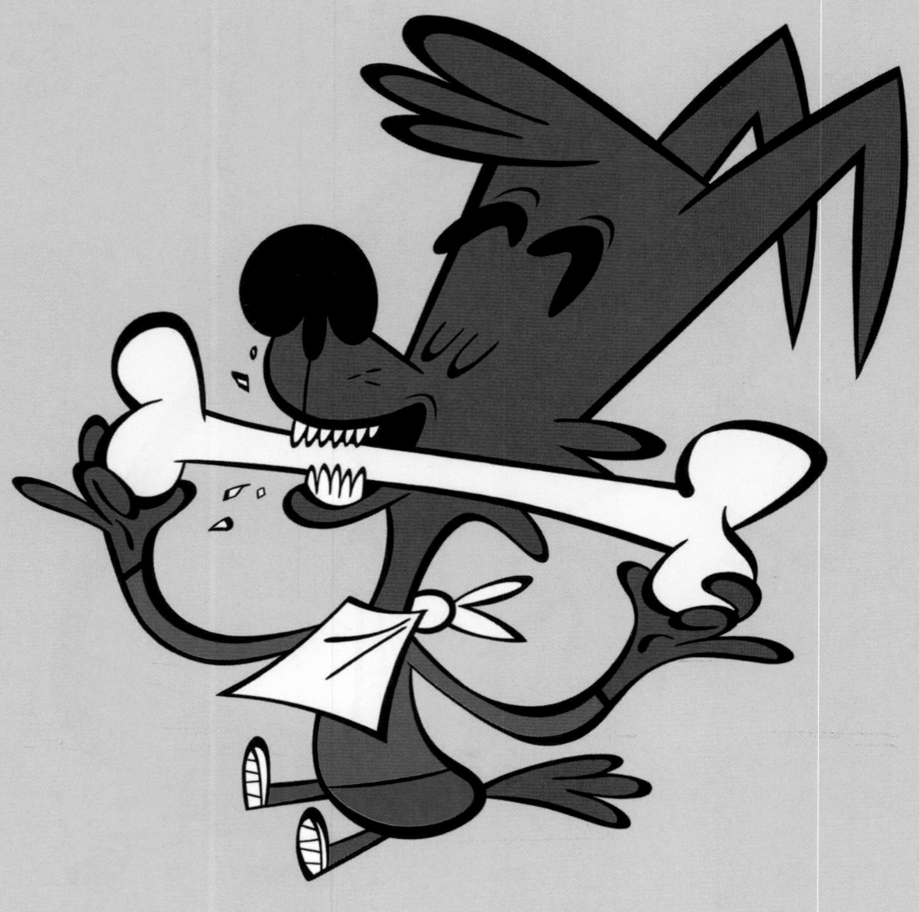

nibble

to take tiny bites of something

Grit **nibbles** a delicious bone.

mrswordsmith.com

eat, sleep, and laugh words

gulp

to swallow a lot all in one go

Bearnice **gulps** an entire pool.

mrswordsmith.com

devour

to eat quickly or hungrily

Plato **devours** the whole pie.

mrswordsmith.com

eat, sleep, and laugh words

tired

when you haven't got any energy left

Oz is too **tired** to have fun on the swings.

mrswordsmith.com

drowsy

when you feel like you are about to fall asleep

Yin and Yang are **drowsy** after drinking the milk.

mrswordsmith.com

exhausted

when you are very tired and worn out

Shang High spills his juice because he is **exhausted**.

mrswordsmith.com

eat, sleep, and laugh words

sleep

what you do when you shut your eyes at night to rest

Grit **sleeps** deeply.

mrswordsmith.com

snore

to make a snorting or grunting sound while you sleep

Bearnice **snores** so loudly that she keeps Bogart awake.

mrswordsmith.com

sleepwalk

to get up and walk about in your sleep

Oz **sleepwalks** across her bedroom.

mrswordsmith.com

laugh

what you do when you find something funny

Yin and Yang **laugh** constantly.

mrswordsmith.com

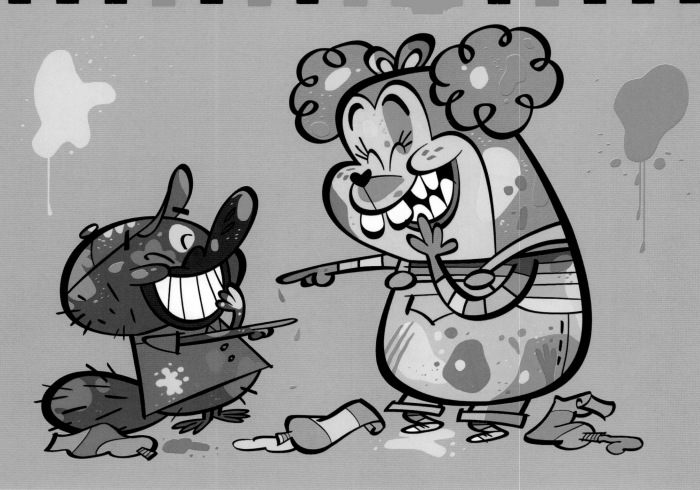

giggle

to laugh in a silly way

Plato and Bearnice **giggle** when they get covered in paint.

mrswordsmith.com

cackle

to laugh in a loud, wild way

Oz **cackles** when she finishes her evil plan.

mrswordsmith.com

funny

something that makes you laugh

Grit wears a **funny** disguise.

mrswordsmith.com

eat, sleep, and laugh words

silly

ridiculous or nonsensical

Armie does something **silly** to make people laugh.

mrswordsmith.com

hysterical

so funny you can't contain yourself

Foot tickles make Bearnice **hysterical**.

mrswordsmith.com

eat, sleep, and laugh words

dream

to close your eyes and imagine a whole other world

Oz **dreams** about winning a prize.

mrswordsmith.com

curious

when you really want to find out more about something

Plato is **curious** about the shell.

mrswordsmith.com

imagine

to use your mind to see the world completely differently

Grit **imagines** he is fighting a huge dragon.

mrswordsmith.com

discover

to find something new or unexpected

Shang High **discovers** Bogart under a rock.

mrswordsmith.com

draw

to create a picture by making lines or marks

Yin and Yang **draw** a tiger in the sand.

mrswordsmith.com

paint

to create a picture with paint

Plato **paints** a picture.

mrswordsmith.com

doodle

to draw or scribble without thinking about it

Bearnice **doodles** when she is bored.

mrswordsmith.com

sculpt

to create a new shape out of something like stone or clay

Oz **sculpts** a statue of herself.

mrswordsmith.com

build

to put things together to make something new

Armie, Oz, and Bogart **build** a sandcastle.

mrswordsmith.com

fix

to put something back together again

Yin and Yang **fix** the broken vase.

mrswordsmith.com

adjust

to move or change something slightly

Shang High **adjusts** the temperature of the shower.

mrswordsmith.com

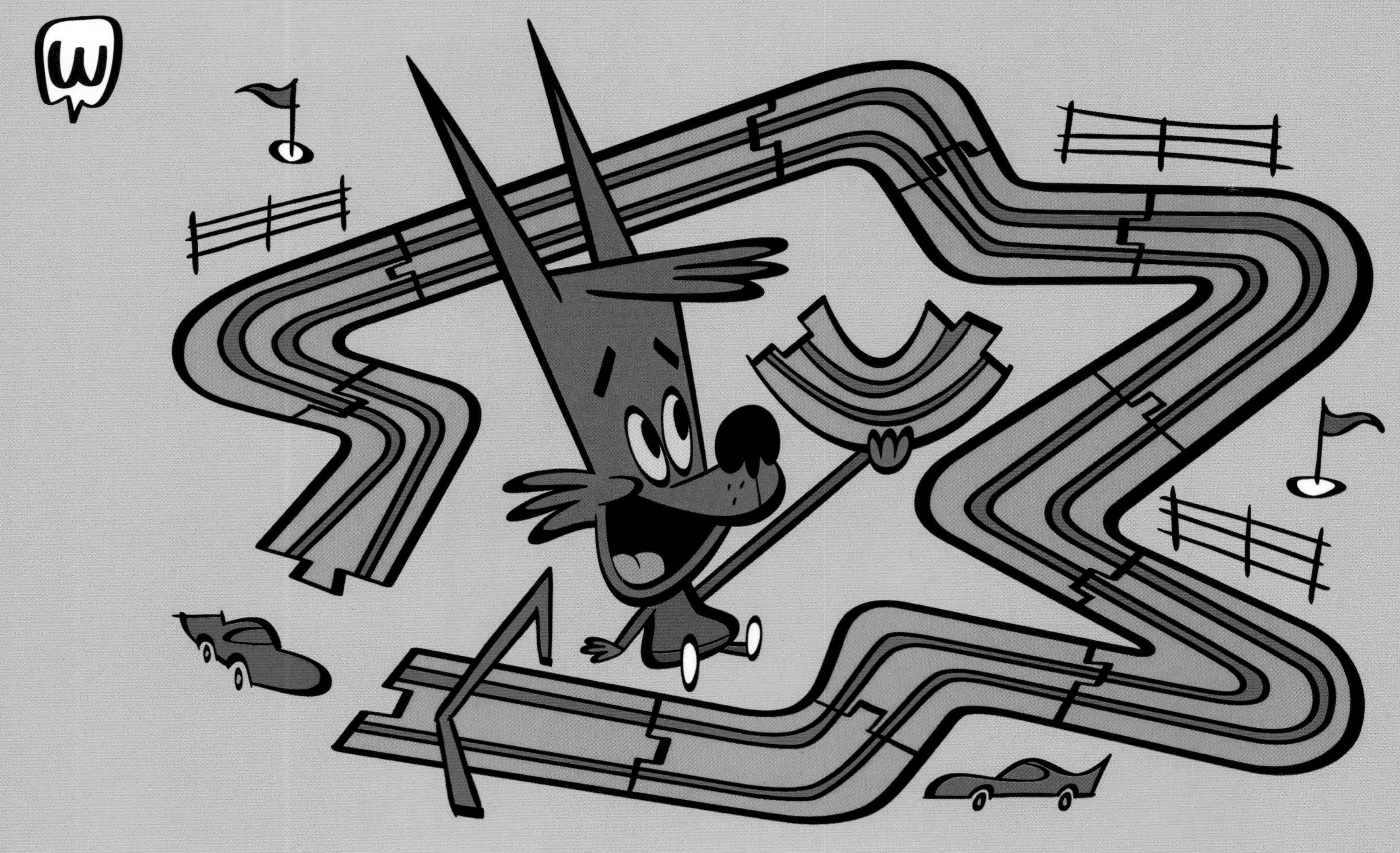

construct

to build or make something

Grit **constructs** a new toy racetrack.

mrswordsmith.com

make

to create or produce

Brick **makes** the best juice.

mrswordsmith.com

invent

to make or think of something new

Armie **invents** a flying machine.

mrswordsmith.com

design

to plan to make something

Oz **designs** a teddy bear.

mrswordsmith.com

concoct

to make by mixing ingredients

Yang and Brick **concoct** a milkshake.

mrswordsmith.com

different

not the same as the others

Oz is **different** from the others.

mrswordsmith.com

unusual

interesting and different from other things

Plato rides an **unusual** bike.

mrswordsmith.com

unique

the only one of its kind

Brick finds a **unique** flower.

mrswordsmith.com

opposite

completely different in every way

Bearnice and Bogart are in **opposite** moods.

mrswordsmith.com

messy

when everything is mixed up and out of place

Grit's room is very **messy**.

mrswordsmith.com

sloppy

when someone is careless or messy

Brick is a **sloppy** eater.

mrswordsmith.com

dirty

when things are not clean

Yin and Yang make the laundry **dirty**.

mrswordsmith.com

jumbled

when things are mixed up or not in the right order

Oz's shoes are **jumbled**.

mrswordsmith.com

wash

to make something cleaner

Yin and Yang **wash** themselves.

mrswordsmith.com

polish

to make something shinier

Plato **polishes** his bill.

mrswordsmith.com

clean or messy words

soak

to leave something in water

Bearnice **soaks** her hair.

mrswordsmith.com

disinfect

to get rid of all the germs

Bearnice **disinfects** her feet.

mrswordsmith.com

shower

to wash yourself under running water

Plato sings while he **showers**.

mrswordsmith.com

clean or messy words

gargle

to wash your mouth and throat

Oz **gargles** every morning.

mrswordsmith.com

MRS wordsmith

slather

to spread something thickly

Bogart **slathers** lotion all over himself.

mrswordsmith.com

scrub

to rub something hard to make it clean

Shang High **scrubs** the back of his neck.

mrswordsmith.com

urgent

when you really need to do something

Oz has an **urgent** need for the toilet.

mrswordsmith.com

relief

the good feeling you get when something unpleasant stops

Armie feels **relief** when he gets to the potty.

mrswordsmith.com

clean or messy words

unroll

to unwrap or unwind something

Yang **unrolls** the toilet paper.

mrswordsmith.com

flush

to clear the toilet with water

Oz **flushes** the toilet.

mrswordsmith.com

shampoo

to wash your hair with special hair soap

Bearnice **shampoos** her hair.

mrswordsmith.com

brush

to neaten your hair by running a brush through it

Grit **brushes** his fur.

mrswordsmith.com

untangle

to get the twists and knots out

Shang High **untangles** his hair.

mrswordsmith.com

rinse

to wash something with water to get rid of the soap or the dirt

Armie **rinses** his body.

mrswordsmith.com

lie

to say something that is not true

Yang **lies** about taking the cookies.

mrswordsmith.com

fib

to tell a lie about something that isn't important

Armie **fibs** about being bitten by a shark.

mrswordsmith.com

exaggerate

to pretend something is more important than it is

Grit **exaggerates** how much his knee hurts.

mrswordsmith.com

cheat

to do something against the rules of a game

Plato **cheats** by distracting Brick.

mrswordsmith.com

trust

to believe in someone or something

Brick **trusts** Armie to catch him.

mrswordsmith.com

truth

something that is real and true

Bearnice tells the **truth** about breaking the vase.

mrswordsmith.com

honest

when you are truthful and people can trust you

Oz is **honest** and gives Brick the money that he dropped.

sincere

when you show your true feelings

Plato gives Bearnice a **sincere** apology.

mrswordsmith.com

mean

when you are unkind or unfair to other people

Armie is **mean** to Shang High.

mrswordsmith.com

nasty

when you are very bad or unpleasant to others

Plato is **nasty** when he steals Brick's lunch.

mrswordsmith.com

cruel

when you do something hurtful on purpose

Yin is **cruel** to Yang.

mrswordsmith.com

selfish

when you only think about yourself and not others

Oz is **selfish** and takes most of Bogart's cake.

mrswordsmith.com

kind

when someone is nice and does nice things

Yang is **kind** when she helps Shang High reach the leaves.

mrswordsmith.com

sensitive

when someone feels everything very deeply

Grit feels **sensitive** when his plant dies.

mrswordsmith.com

considerate

when you do something for someone else out of kindness

Plato is **considerate** so he helps Bogart cross the road.

mrswordsmith.com

sympathetic

when you understand how somebody feels and you comfort them

Brick is **sympathetic** when Armie's glasses break.

mrswordsmith.com

awesome

when something is amazing or incredible

Shang High's star-surfing is **awesome**.

mrswordsmith.com

amazing

when something is surprising or astonishing

Oz's trick is **amazing**.

mrswordsmith.com

impressive

when something is really good or awesome

Plato can fit an **impressive** number of cookies in his mouth.

mrswordsmith.com

extraordinary

when something is incredible or very unusual

Bogart shows **extraordinary** strength.

mrswordsmith.com

respect

to treat others with appreciation and behave politely

Oz **respects** the rules.

mrswordsmith.com

easygoing

when you feel relaxed and nothing bothers you

Brick is **easygoing** so he lets Yang sleep on him.

mrswordsmith.com

accepting

when you let people be whoever they want to be

Plato and Bearnice are **accepting** of Bogart.

mrswordsmith.com

tolerate

to put up with things that you don't like

Bearnice **tolerates** having her hair pulled.

mrswordsmith.com

feel

to experience something

The film makes Armie **feel** sad.

mrswordsmith.com

zen words

relate

to understand someone because you have things in common

Grit can **relate** to Shang High's broken leg.

mrswordsmith.com

pity

a feeling of sadness or sympathy for another person

Oz feels **pity** for Bogart.

mrswordsmith.com

empathy

the ability to understand other people's feelings

Shang High feels **empathy** for the tree.

mrswordsmith.com

calm

when you feel still and relaxed

Grit stays **calm** despite the bees.

mrswordsmith.com

relax

when you take it easy and rest

Bearnice **relaxes** in her hammock.

mrswordsmith.com

breathe

to fill your lungs with air and let it out

Yin and Yang **breathe** fresh air.

mrswordsmith.com

balance

to stand without wobbling or falling over

Brick **balances** on his surfboard.

mrswordsmith.com

listen

to pay attention when someone speaks

Yin and Yang **listen** to Bogart's story.

mrswordsmith.com

understand

to know how something works

Bearnice **understands** how to tie her shoelaces.

mrswordsmith.com

focus

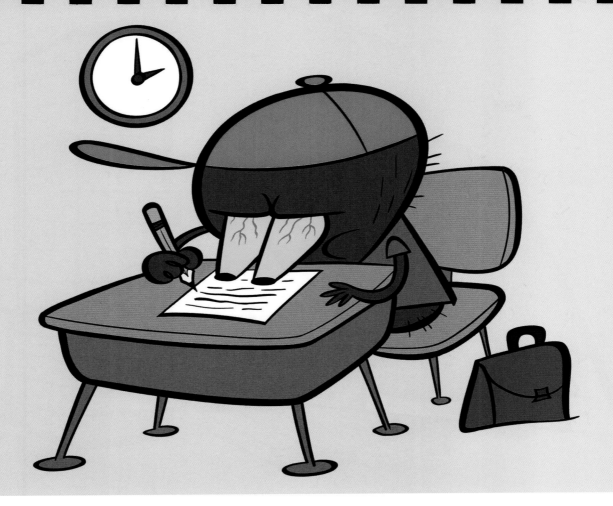

to think about something without getting distracted

Plato **focuses** on the test.

mrswordsmith.com

concentrate

to think very hard about something

Brick **concentrates** so that he doesn't knock over the tower.

mrswordsmith.com

think

what your brain does all the time

Bearnice **thinks** about where to put her block.

mrswordsmith.com

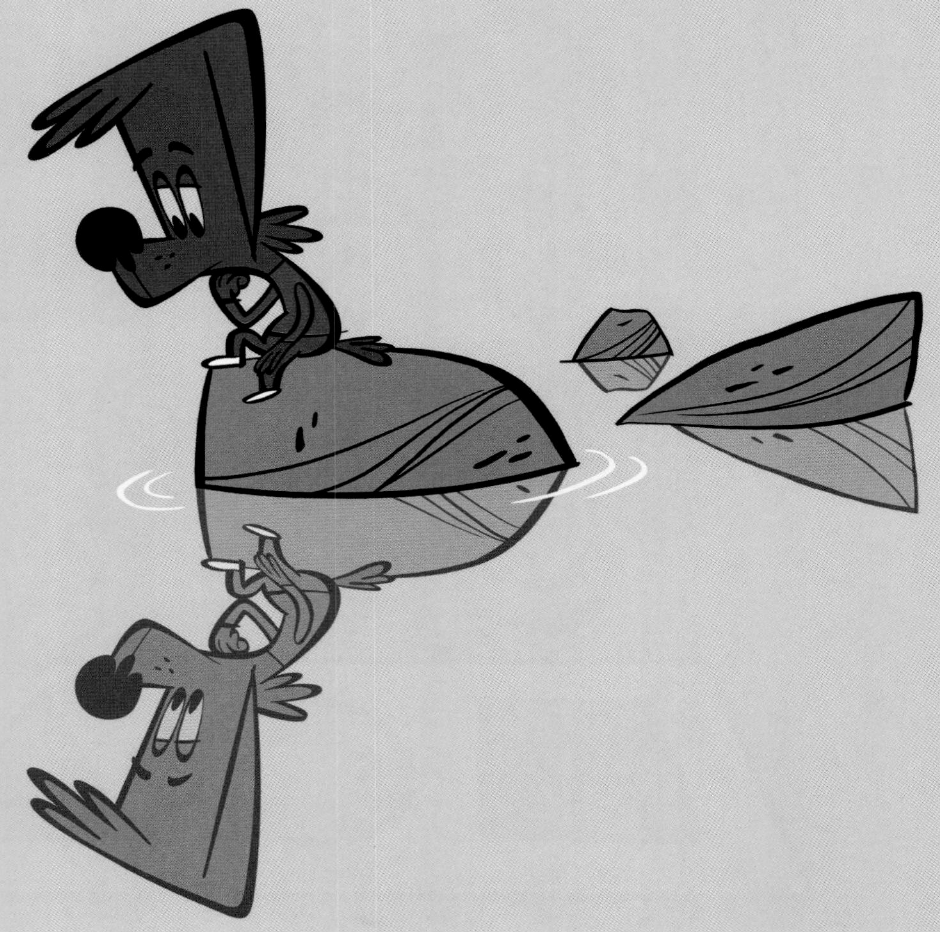

reflect

to think about things that have happened

Grit **reflects** on his life.

mrswordsmith.com

daydream

to imagine nice things

Brick looks at the sky and **daydreams**.

mrswordsmith.com

thoughtful

when you take time to think about other people

Shang High is **thoughtful** so he keeps Plato dry.

mrswordsmith.com

fun

enjoyment, entertainment, or pleasure

Bearnice is having a lot of **fun**.

mrswordsmith.com

carefree

when you are not worried about anything

Plato feels completely **carefree**.

mrswordsmith.com

reckless

when you do something without thinking about how dangerous it could be

Grit does a **reckless** trick on his bike.

mrswordsmith.com

spontaneous

when things happen without being planned

Armie goes for a **spontaneous** swim.

mrswordsmith.com

passion

a strong liking or love for something

Shang High has a **passion** for painting.

mrswordsmith.com

intense

something done with great effort

Yin and Yang have an **intense** staring contest.

mrswordsmith.com

energy

the ability to be active

Oz has enough **energy** to bounce all day long.

mrswordsmith.com

enthusiatic

when you are very excited to do something

Brick is an **enthusiastic** fan of Plato.

mrswordsmith.com

risky

when something could go well or it could go badly

Plato’s decision to press the button is **risky**.

mrswordsmith.com

harmful

when something causes hurt or pain

Bogart accidentally breathes in the **harmful** car fumes.

mrswordsmith.com

dangerous

when something is not safe

Yang should not bite the wire because it is very **dangerous**.

mrswordsmith.com

threatening

when something is scary or intimidating

Brick is a **threatening** opponent.

mrswordsmith.com

explore

to search and discover things

Yin and Yang **explore** the ocean.

mrswordsmith.com

seek

to look for something

Shang High **seeks** the truth.

mrswordsmith.com

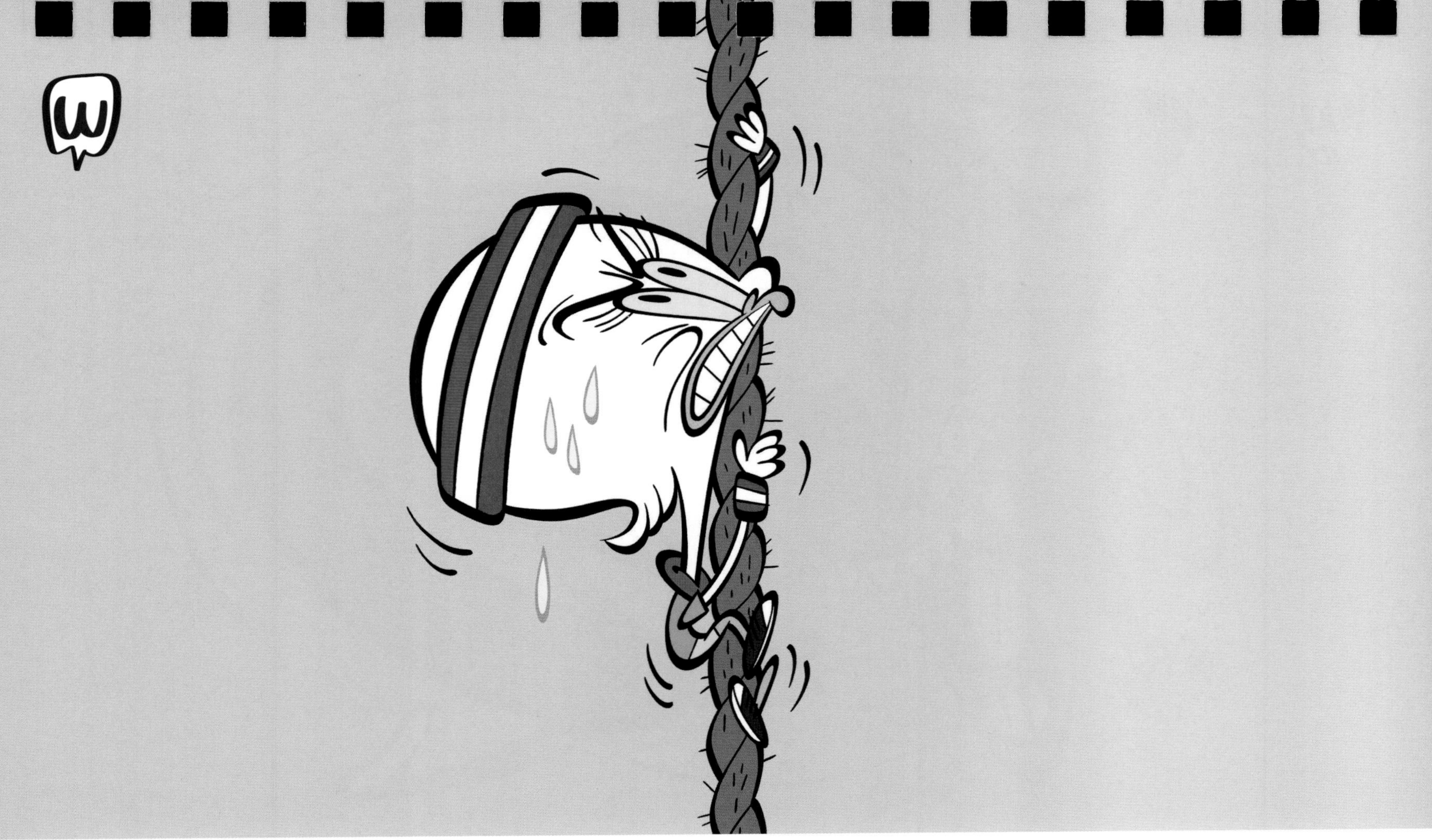

climb

to go up or get to the top of something

Oz **climbs** up the rope.

mrswordsmith.com

chase

to hurry after something and try to catch it

Grit **chases** his tail.

mrswordsmith.com

lead

to have others follow you

Brick **leads** the mice.

mrswordsmith.com

guide

to show people the way

Grit **guides** his friends.

mrswordsmith.com

influence

to change the way other people act

Oz **influences** her friends.

mrswordsmith.com

inspire

to make someone excited to do something

Books **inspire** Armie to go on adventures.

mrswordsmith.com

scared

when you feel frightened or afraid

Oz is **scared** of being so high up.

mrswordsmith.com

spooked

how you feel when something scary surprises you

Yang is **spooked** when she sees the spider.

mrswordsmith.com

jittery

when you feel nervous and can't relax

Plato is a **jittery** flyer.

mrswordsmith.com

nightmare

a scary or upsetting dream

Bogart has a **nightmare** about scary fish.

mrswordsmith.com

safe and scared words

shout

to speak loudly or make a loud noise

Grit is very rude and **shouts** at Plato.

mrswordsmith.com

scream

to make a long, high-pitched cry

Yin **screams** when she sees Bearnice.

mrswordsmith.com

shriek

to make a short, loud cry

Bearnice **shrieks** when she opens the box.

mrswordsmith.com

squeal

to make a long, high-pitched noise

Oz **squeals** when she sees the gift.

mrswordsmith.com

hide

to cover something up so that no one sees it

Yang **hides** under the rug.

mrswordsmith.com

secret

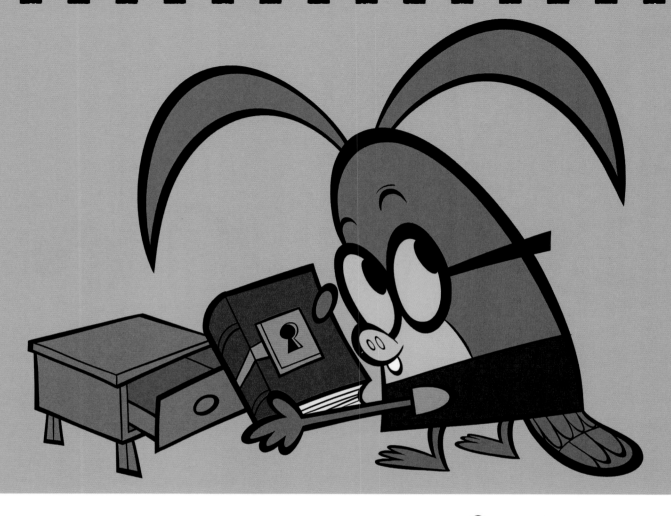

something that you don't tell people

Armie has a **secret**.

mrswordsmith.com

bury

to put something in a hole and cover it

Oz **buries** her head in the sand.

mrswordsmith.com

disguise

to hide your face or dress up as someone else

Shang High wears a **disguise**.

mrswordsmith.com

hug

to squeeze someone in your arms to show you care

Yin and Yang **hug** Brick.

mrswordsmith.com

cuddle

to hold someone in your arms in a loving way

Grit **cuddles** his bone.

mrswordsmith.com

snuggle

to move your body into a warm, comfortable position

Oz **snuggles** with her teddy bear.

mrswordsmith.com

huddle

to crowd closely together with other people

Everyone **huddles** together around the campfire.

mrswordsmith.com

safe

to be free from harm or danger

Shang High feels **safe** because he is wearing lots of protective gear.

mrswordsmith.com

secure

to be free from danger or risk

Armie feels **secure** because he is wearing lots of seat belts.

mrswordsmith.com

comfortable

to feel relaxed and at ease

Bearnice feels **comfortable** in her big, soft armchair.

mrswordsmith.com

harmless

something that isn't dangerous or likely to cause harm

Brick knows that the spider is **harmless**.

mrswordsmith.com

hard

something that is not easy

Armie finds the **puzzle** hard.

mrswordsmith.com

difficult

something that you find really hard

It's **difficult** for Bearnice to pull the sword free.

mrswordsmith.com

effort words

tricky

something that takes a lot of skill and practice

Shang High finds juggling **tricky**.

mrswordsmith.com

tough

something that is difficult and takes a lot of effort

Armie's training is **tough**.

mrswordsmith.com

effort words

confused

when you don't understand or you can't think clearly

Grit is **confused** by the complicated signs.

mrswordsmith.com

baffled

when you feel like something doesn't make any sense

Yin and Yang are **baffled** by the stranger who looks like them.

mrswordsmith.com

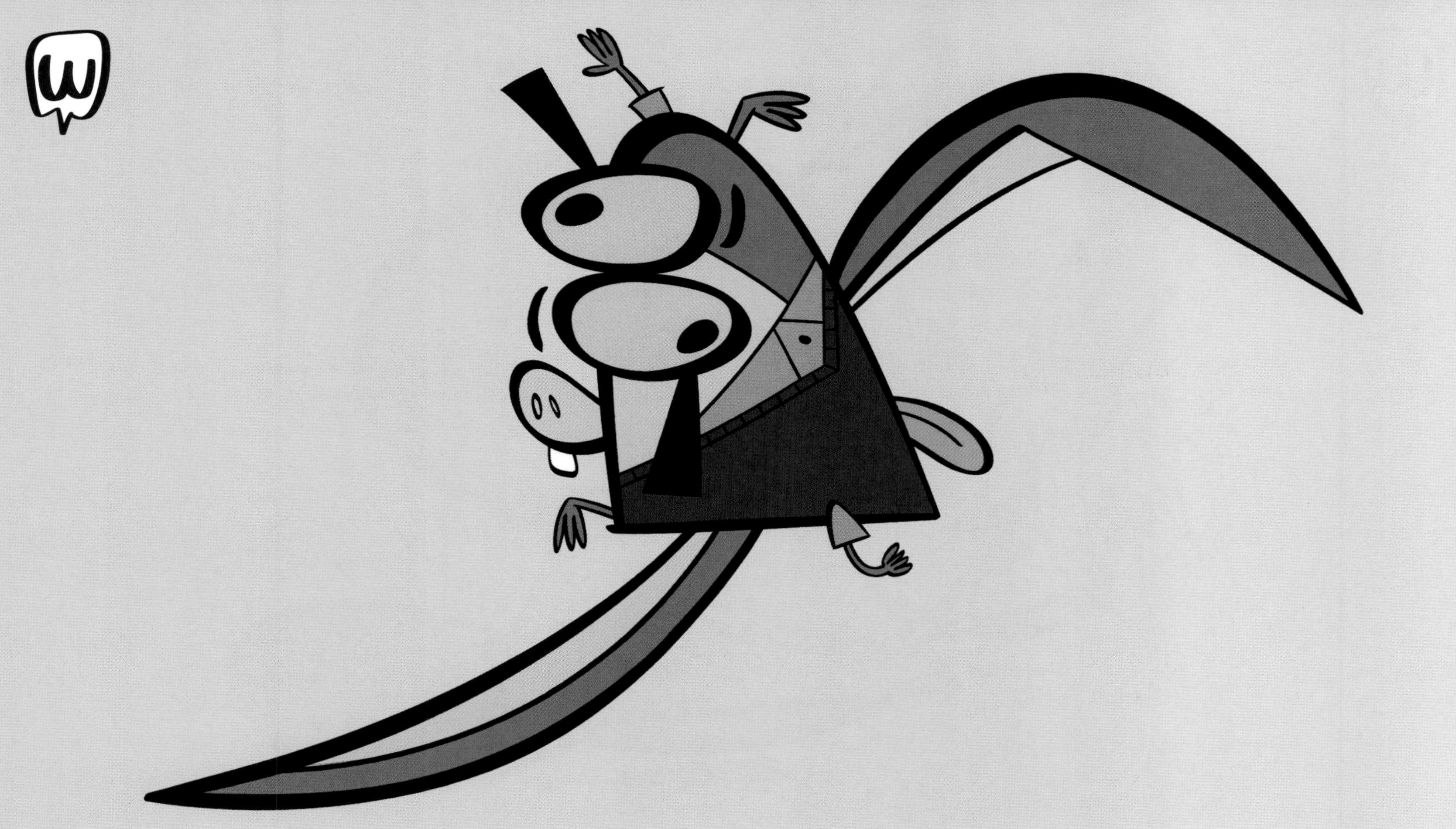

muddled

when everything is mixed up and the wrong way around

Armie feels **muddled**.

mrswordsmith.com

puzzled

when you can't work out how something happened

Plato is **puzzled** when he finds a sausage in a banana peel.

mrswordsmith.com

practice

doing something again and again so you get better at it

Armie has a lot of **practice** making paper boats.

mrswordsmith.com

habit

something you do often without having to think about it

Grit makes a **habit** of brushing his teeth.

mrswordsmith.com

repeat

to do something again

Yin **repeats** Yang's skating pattern.

mrswordsmith.com

fail

to try to do something and get it wrong

Shang High **fails** to put on his hoodie properly.

mrswordsmith.com

try

when you make an effort to do something

Yin and Yang **try** to catch a star.

mrswordsmith.com

effort

when you really try to do something

Shang High makes a big **effort** to blow out the candles.

mrswordsmith.com

struggle

something that is difficult to do

The tug-of-war between Oz and Armie is a **struggle**.

mrswordsmith.com

persevere

to keep going even when it is difficult

Brick **perseveres** with his exercises.

mrswordsmith.com

problem

something that has gone wrong and needs fixing

Plato has a **problem** when he runs out of toilet paper.

mrswordsmith.com

solution

a way to fix or solve a problem

Brick finds the **solution** to the puzzle.

mrswordsmith.com

mistake

something that goes wrong by accident

Plato makes a **mistake** and puts the record in the dishwasher.

mrswordsmith.com

challenge

something that is difficult to do or finish

Grit likes the **challenge** of climbing the wall.

mrswordsmith.com

friends

people who get along well and love each other

Oz and Bearnice are **friends**.

mrswordsmith.com

family

a group of people who love and take care of each other

Brick goes out for a walk with his **family**.

mrswordsmith.com

team

a group of people who work together to do something

The animals form a rowing **team**.

mrswordsmith.com

ignore

to take no notice of someone or something

Oz **ignores** the sign on the beach.

mrswordsmith.com

exclude

to leave someone out

Grit and Bogart **exclude** Shang High from their joke.

mrswordsmith.com

neglect

to forget about something and stop looking after it

Oz **neglects** her plant.

mrswordsmith.com

reject

to strongly say no to something

Bearnice **rejects** all broccoli.

mrswordsmith.com

like

to have a good feeling about something or someone

Grit **likes** ice cream.

mrswordsmith.com

love

to have very strong affection for something or someone

Yin and Yang **love** each other.

mrswordsmith.com

adore

to love someone and think they are very special

Bearnice **adores** Bogart.

mrswordsmith.com

obsessed

when you think about something or someone all the time

Armie is **obsessed** with his new video game.

mrswordsmith.com

share

to do something with other people

Shang High **shares** a hotdog with his friends.

mrswordsmith.com

include

to let everyone join in

Bearnice **includes** Grit in movie night.

mrswordsmith.com

together

when you do something with another person

The friends carry the fridge **together**.

mrswordsmith.com

collaborate

to work together

Yin and Yang **collaborate** to build a snowman.

mrswordsmith.com

help

to make something easier for someone

Oz **helps** Brick by giving him a life ring.

mrswordsmith.com

save

to keep safe or rescue

Brick **saves** Yin and Yang from the tree.

mrswordsmith.com

fasten

to close or buckle securely

Brick **fastens** his seatbelt.

mrswordsmith.com

comfort

to soothe someone or make them feel better

Plato **comforts** Armie.

mrswordsmith.com

smirk

to smile in a mean way

Yang **smirks** when she steals Yin's teddy bear.

mrswordsmith.com

break

to separate into pieces with force

Armie **breaks** his pencil.

mrswordsmith.com

destroy

to completely ruin something

Grit and Bogart **destroy** the sofa.

mrswordsmith.com

tantrum words

ruin

to spoil or destroy

Bearnice **ruins** the cake.

mrswordsmith.com

shatter

to break into lots of little pieces

Oz **shatters** the mirror.

mrswordsmith.com

moody

when you feel sad one moment and happy the next

Plato feels very **moody**.

mrswordsmith.com

tantrum

when someone is crying, shouting, and out of control

Brick has a **tantrum** and bangs his fists on the ground.

mrswordsmith.com

grumpy

when you are in a bad mood

Armie feels **grumpy** in the morning.

mrswordsmith.com

tantrum words

frustrated

when you feel annoyed and can't stand it anymore

Oz is **frustrated** when the cards collapse.

mrswordsmith.com

cry

what you do when you're sad and tears fall from your eyes

Yin and Yang **cry** about the spilled milk.

mrswordsmith.com

sob

to cry noisily with loud gasps

Bearnice **sobs** until her head hurts.

mrswordsmith.com

blubber

to cry uncontrollably and loudly

Plato **blubbers** for so long that his house fills with tears.

mrswordsmith.com

wail

when you get upset and cry out with a long, high noise

Armie **wails** when his toy is taken away.

mrswordsmith.com

frown

a sad expression with your eyebrows pushed down

Oz has a **frown** on her face.

mrswordsmith.com

pout

to stick your lips out in a moody way

Armie **pouts** and crosses his arms.

mrswordsmith.com

scowl

to frown in an angry or bad-tempered way

Grit **scowls** at the camera.

mrswordsmith.com

sulk

to be quiet, and grumpy, and mope about

Brick **sulks** when he doesn't get his way.

mrswordsmith.com

sorry

when you feel sad or regretful

Yin said **sorry** for accidentally hitting Grit with a baseball.

mrswordsmith.com

apology

a way of showing that you are sorry

Brick makes an **apology** to Armie for dropping his ice cream.

forgive

to stop feeling angry towards someone

Bearnice **forgives** Yang for eating her cookies.

mrswordsmith.com

regret

when you feel bad and wish you hadn't done something

"I **regret** eating so many doughnuts," says Plato.

mrswordsmith.com

excited

when you feel a lot of enthusiasm and energy

Grit is **excited** by what he sees on TV.

mrswordsmith.com

impatient

when you can't wait for something to happen

Bogart is **impatient** to eat pizza.

mrswordsmith.com

eager

when you really want to do something

Shang High is **eager** to eat ice cream.

mrswordsmith.com

thrilled

when you are very happy and excited

Armie is **thrilled** when the rocket takes off.

mrswordsmith.com

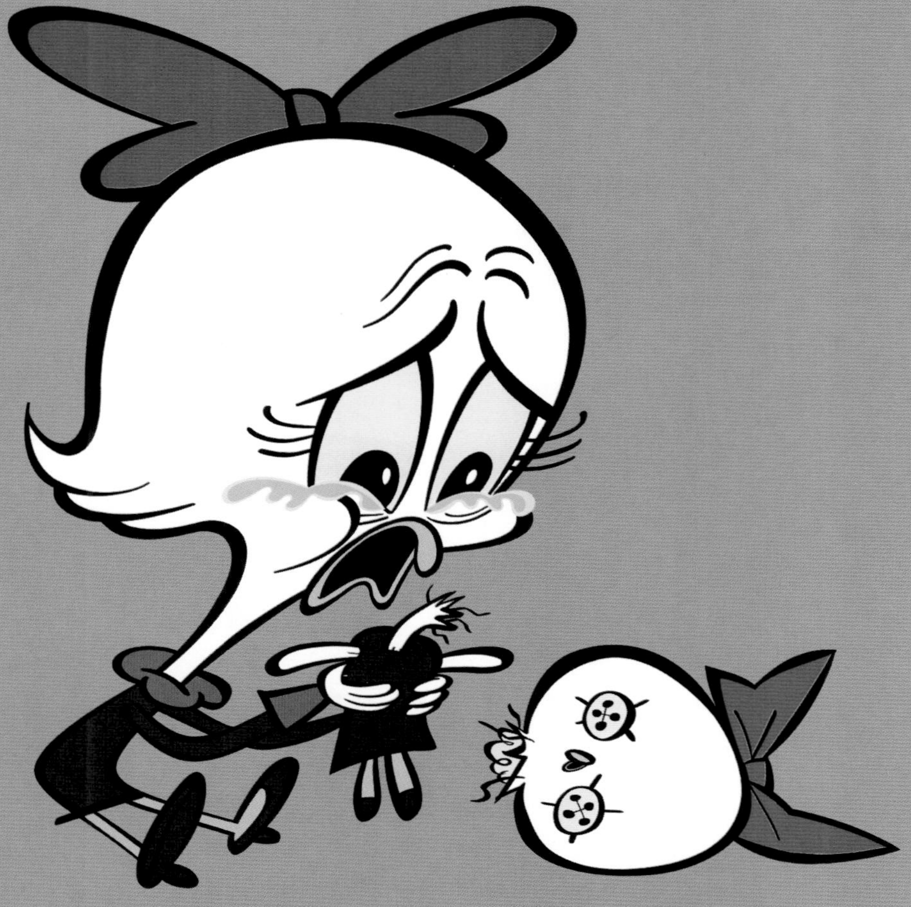

hurt

how you feel when someone does something mean

Oz feels **hurt** because her doll is torn.

mrswordsmith.com

upset

how you feel if you are sad or worried about something

Bearnice is **upset** because her skateboard is broken.

mrswordsmith.com

jealous

how you feel when you want something that someone else has

Yin is **jealous** of her sister's trophy.

mrswordsmith.com

insulted

how you feel when someone does something rude

Shang High is **insulted** by Grit's ugly painting.

mrswordsmith.com

sad

when you feel unhappy

Yin and Yang are **sad** when they lose their balloon.

mrswordsmith.com

heartbroken

when something makes you very upset and sad

Oz is so **heartbroken** that she falls to the floor.

mrswordsmith.com

miserable

when you feel very unhappy or uncomfortable

The cold bath makes Yin and Yang **miserable**.

mrswordsmith.com

disappointed

how you feel when something isn't as good as you expected

Oz is **disappointed** with her birthday present.

mrswordsmith.com

angry

when you have a strong feeling against something

Oz is so **angry** that she might explode.

mrswordsmith.com

annoyed

when you feel a little bit angry

Armie is **annoyed** with Brick for being silly.

mrswordsmith.com

disapproving

when you think something is wrong and you show it

Bearnice **disapproves** when Yin draws on the wall.

mrswordsmith.com

fuming

when you feel lots of anger building up inside

Plato is so angry that he is **fuming**.

mrswordsmith.com

happy

when you feel full of joy

Brick and Grit feel **happy** in the pool.

mrswordsmith.com

cheerful

when you are in a very good mood

Yin and Yang do a **cheerful** dance.

mrswordsmith.com

blissful

when you are completely happy in every way

Bearnice feels **blissful** on the grass.

mrswordsmith.com

elated

when you are so happy you feel like you could fly

Shang High feels **elated** after making a friend.

mrswordsmith.com

nervous

when you are scared or unsure about something

Armie is **nervous** about going down the slide.

mrswordsmith.com

worried

when you are afraid that something will go wrong

Bearnice is **worried** that Bogart will fall and hurt himself.

mrswordsmith.com

anxious

when you are worried about what might happen

Oz is **anxious** about getting into the pool.

mrswordsmith.com

tense

when you feel stressed or under pressure

Grit is **tense** because he wants to win.

mrswordsmith.com

shy

when you feel nervous around other people

Brick feels **shy** at parties.

mrswordsmith.com

timid

when you don't feel brave or confident

Shang High feels **timid** when he meets new friends.

mrswordsmith.com

quiet

when there is very little noise and nothing to disturb you

Plato finds a **quiet** spot to relax in.

mrswordsmith.com

embarrassed

when you feel ashamed and just want to hide

Grit feels **embarrassed** when his trousers rip.

mrswordsmith.com

speak

to say something out loud

Yin and Yang **speak** into the string telephone.

mrswordsmith.com

contribute

to give something or help out

Grit **contributes** money to charity.

mrswordsmith.com

volunteer

to put yourself forward to do something

Oz **volunteers** to answer the question.

mrswordsmith.com

join

to become part of a group or start doing something

Oz **joins** the water fight.

mrswordsmith.com

confident

when you feel sure of yourself and what you can do

Oz is **confident** that she can fly.

mrswordsmith.com

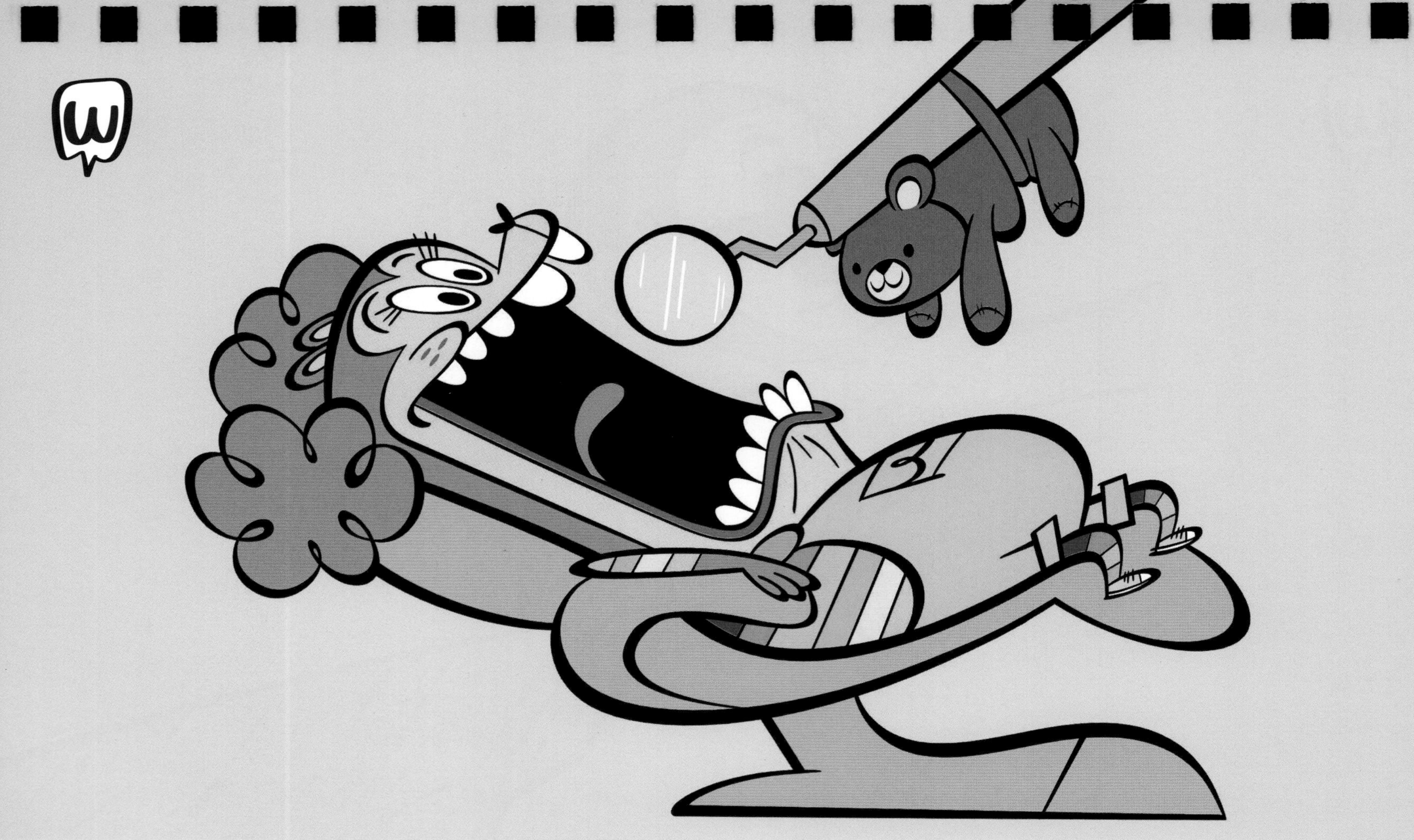

brave

when you are ready to do something that scares you

Bearnice is **brave** when she visits the dentist.

mrswordsmith.com

bold

when you are ready to take risks or do risky things

Armie has **bold** plans.

mrswordsmith.com

courageous

when you are not scared away by danger

Brick is **courageous** when he saves people.

mrswordsmith.com

wait

to pause until something is ready

Brick and Plato **wait** to use the toilet.

mrswordsmith.com

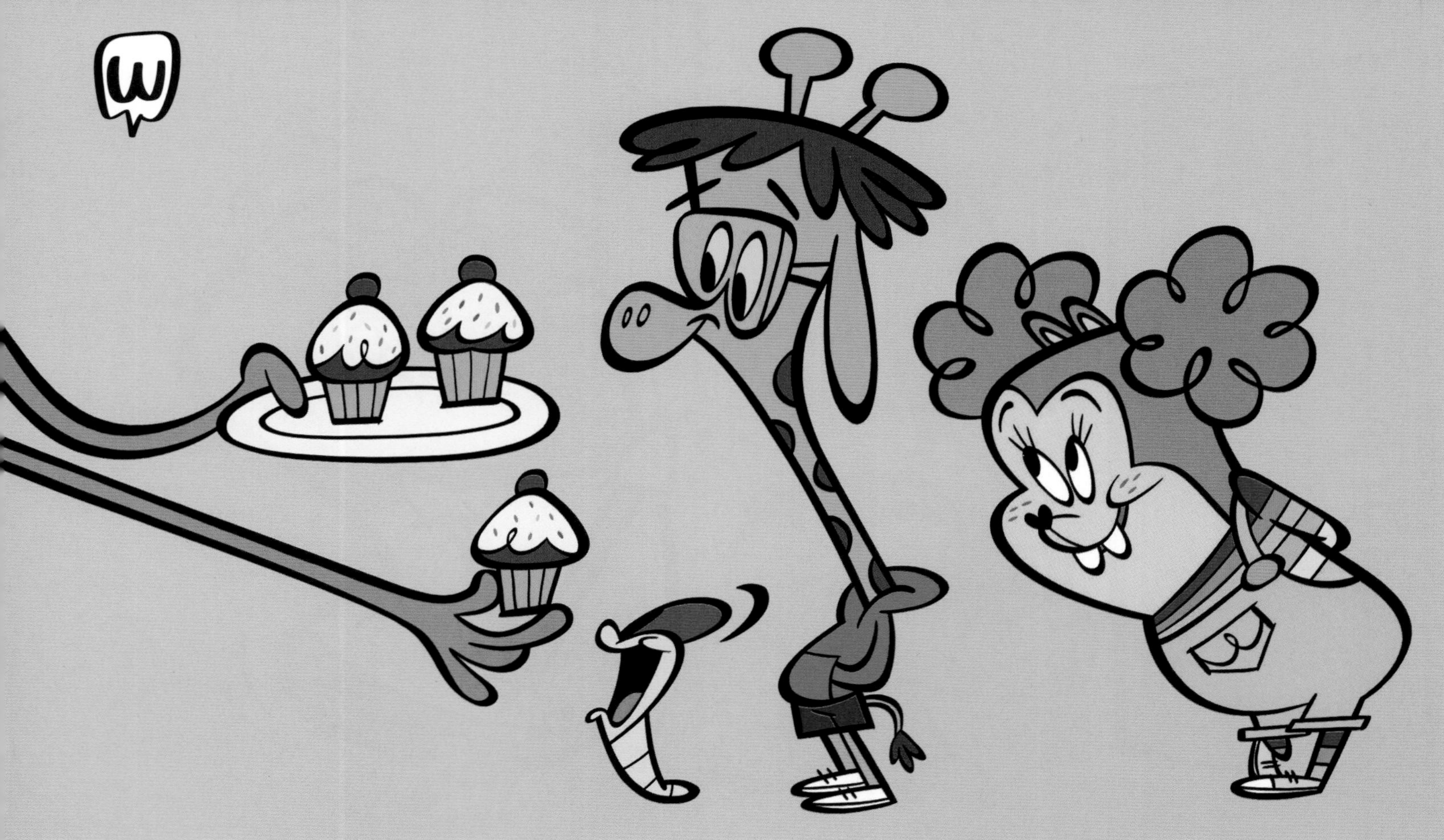

patient

when you wait calmly for something

Bearnice is **patient** as she waits for a cupcake.

mrswordsmith.com

polite

when you behave in a respectful way

Oz is very **polite** to her friend.

mrswordsmith.com

cooperate

to help someone or work together

Yin and Yang **cooperate** to get the cookies.

mrswordsmith.com